WEEKLY WR READER®
EARLY LEARNING LIBRARY

Where People Work

What Happens at a
Recycling Center?

by Kathleen Pohl

Reading consultant: Susan Nations, M.Ed., author/literacy coach/consultant in literacy development

Please visit our web site at: www.garethstevens.com
For a free color catalog describing Weekly Reader® Early Learning Library's list
of high-quality books, call 1-877-445-5824 (USA) or 1-800-387-3178 (Canada).
Weekly Reader® Early Learning Library's fax: (414) 336-0164.

Library of Congress Cataloging-in-Publication Data

Pohl, Kathleen.
    What happens at a recycling center? / by Kathleen Pohl.
      p. cm. — (Where people work)
    Includes bibliographical references and index.
    ISBN-10: 0-8368-6888-9 — ISBN-13: 978-0-8368-6888-3 (lib. bdg.)
    ISBN-10: 0-8368-6895-1 — ISBN-13: 978-0-8368-6895-1 (softcover)
    1. Recycling (Waste, etc.)—Juvenile literature.   2. Recycling centers—Juvenile literature.
I. Title. II. Series: Pohl, Kathleen. Where people work.
TD792.P64   2007
363.72'82—dc22   2006009111

This edition first published in 2007 by
Weekly Reader® Early Learning Library
A Member of the WRC Media Family of Companies
330 West Olive Street, Suite 100
Milwaukee, WI 53212 USA

Managing editor: Dorothy L. Gibbs
Art direction: Tammy West
Cover design and page layout: Scott M. Krall
Picture research: Diane Laska-Swanke and Kathleen Pohl
Photographer: Jack Long

Acknowledgments: The publisher thanks Brittany, Brooke, and Dana Bebo and Mary Jo Ward
and Jim Molenda for modeling in this book. Special thanks to Mary Jo and John Ward, of
National Salvage, Ltd., for their expert consulting and the use of their company's facilities.

Printed in the United States of America

1 2 3 4 5 6 7 8 9 10 09 08 07 06

Hi, Kids!

I'm Buddy, your Weekly Reader® pal. Have you ever visited a recycling center? I'm here to show and tell what happens at a recycling center. So, come on. Turn the page and read along!

Do you know what this sign means? That's right. It means **recycle**! It tells us we should not throw away things we can use again. When we recycle, we help save Earth.

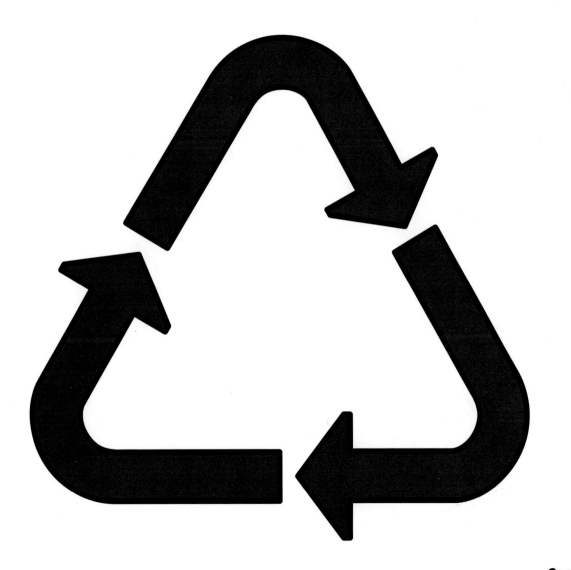

Brittany and Brooke are at a recycling center. They have some empty metal cans. Most of the cans are **aluminum**.

Mrs. Ward works at the recycling center. She uses a **magnet** to find cans that are not aluminum. **Steel** cans stick to the magnet. Aluminum cans do not.

magnet

Mrs. Ward weighs the cans on a big **scale**. Now she knows how much to pay Brittany and Brooke for them.

control for scale

scale

Jim is Mrs. Ward's helper.
He runs a big machine.
Jim dumps Brittany and
Brooke's cans into a bin
called a **hopper**.

hopper

13

A **conveyor belt** carries the cans from the hopper to a can crusher. The crusher smashes the cans flat.

conveyor belt

can crusher

hopper

15

The crusher also presses the cans into small squares. They are called **biscuits**. Hundreds of cans are in each biscuit.

biscuit

Jim makes big stacks of biscuits. The stacks are called **bricks**. Stacks of crushed cans are used to make new cans!

You can recycle cans, too! Do you have a recycling center near you?

Recycling a Can

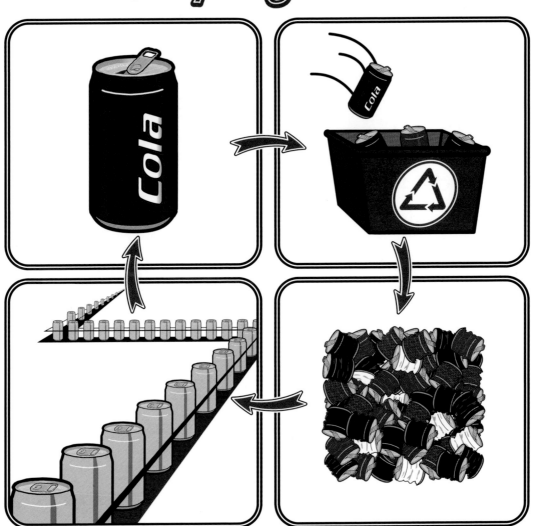

🐻 Glossary

aluminum — a soft, lightweight metal that is used to make drink cans and many other products

conveyor belt — part of a machine that looks like a wide, flat belt and is used to move objects along in a line

magnet — a piece of metal with a special power to make iron or steel move toward it and stick to it

recyle — to use old materials to make new materials

steel — a hard, strong metal made of iron

🐻 For More Information

Books

Recycle! A Handbook for Kids. Gail Gibbons (Little, Brown)

Recycling a Can. Cynthia MacGregor (Rosen)

Spyglass Books: Waste Not. Rebecca Weber (Compass Point Books)

Web Site

Jimmy Neutron's Recycling Mission
www.recycleyourcans.org
Enjoy Jimmy and Goddard's video about how to recycle cans, then launch their recycling mission to learn a lot more about recycling.

Publisher's note to educators and parents: Our editors have carefully reviewed this Web site to ensure that it is suitable for children. Many Web sites change frequently, however, and we cannot guarantee that a site's future contents will continue to meet our high standards of quality and educational value. Be advised that children should be closely supervised whenever they access the Internet.

# Index

About the Author

Kathleen Pohl has written and edited many children's books. Among them are animal tales, rhyming books, retold classics, and the forty-book series *Nature Close-Ups*. She also served for many years as top editor of *Taste of Home* and *Country Woman* magazines. She and her husband, Bruce, live among beautiful Wisconsin woods and share their home with six goats, a llama, and all kinds of wonderful woodland creatures.